EXODUS REVISITED

Other works by LEON URIS

Novels: Battle Cry • The Angry Hills • Exodus

Screenplays: Battle Cry • Gunfight at the O.K. Corral

Text by LEON URIS

Photography by DIMITRIOS HARISSIADIS

Project coordination by ILAN HARTUV

Exodus Revisited

by LEON URIS
and DIMITRIOS HARISSIADIS

Doubleday & Company, Inc., Garden City, New York

Library of Congress Catalog Card Number 60-13085
Copyright © 1959, 1960 by Leon Uris and Dimitrios Harissiadis
All Rights Reserved
Printed in the United States of America
Designed by Alma Reese Cardi
First Edition

There is an old Yemenite folk tale that
David has returned to Israel.
He has.
This book is dedicated to DAVID BEN GURION.

CONTENTS

Book One

Israel is a land of contrasts.

12

Liberated slaves fled Egypt and wandered into the Wilderness of Zin and Paran and Etham. They passed through the Red Sea and drifted in the bleakness for four long and bitter decades in search of their promised oasis.

Throughout their ordeal, they raised hope-filled voices and found an eternal expression of man's relationship to God. The Jewish people gave to a groping mankind its first great bridge from darkness to light.

Beatitudes, on the Sea of Galilee . . . The Sermon on the Mount. A universal message for all men of all times.

The people of Israel gave us our greatest moral cornerstone, *monotheism*. From Judaism emerged Christianity.

"And seeing the multitudes, He went up into a mountain . . . Blessed are the meek, for they shall inherit the earth."

20

The pageantry of Christianity is everywhere in Israel. Kfar Kana, site of the first miracle, the changing of water to wine at the wedding.

A monastery on Mount Tabor marks the traditional site of the Trans-figuration.

Ein Karem, birthplace of John the Baptist.

At Capernaum, Jesus preached in a synagogue to his fellow Jews.

The site of the Miracle of Loaves and Fishes is adorned by this Byzantine mosaic.

Nazareth . . .

26

Fishermen on the Sea of Galilee mend their nets in the timeless way another Fisherman must have mended his.

"Deep river . . . my home is over Jordan."

Israel is the common heritage of Jew, Christian, and Moslem. Mount Carmel, where the Prophet Elijah battled the evil priests of Jezebel, is sacred to three religions.

From Judaism and Christianity a third great religion was born. Islam!
The submission to God's will.
"There is no God, but God."

The Mosque of Omar stands on another place sacred to three religions. On the site of the Temple, Mohammed ascended to heaven and obtained the wisdom of Solomon.

Are we not but branches of the same tree? There are many ways to express the same idea. Those who follow the teachings of Bahai have their way.

The Roman Catholic Church has its way . . .

. . . and the Russian Orthodox Church has its.

Archbishop Isidoros is the leader of the Greek Church.

34

At the Church of the Annunciation in Nazareth the Greek Orthodox
ritual is conducted in Arabic.

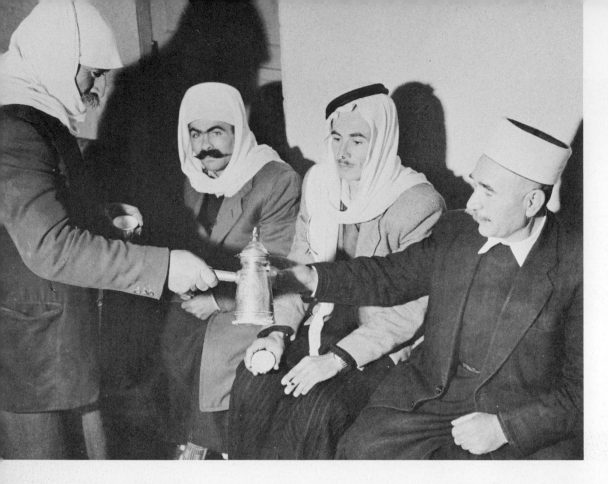

The Druses consider Jethro, the father-in-law of Moses, their Chief Prophet.

Behind the curtain are the oldest Torah scrolls in Israel.

36

The Emperor of Ethiopia calls himself "The Lion of Judah," and the Abyssinian Church has its way, too. The conclusion is the same: "The Lord is our God. The Lord is *one*."

After the centuries of golden history recorded in our Bible, the Second Temple was destroyed. Later revolutionaries continued the battle. No people on earth ever fought more furiously for their freedom. Simon Bar Kochba, one of the greatest, brought his men down from the Judean hills and nearly swept the legions of Rome from the land.

What monument to glory is greater than the fortress of Masada? Two hundred and eighty-six Jews held back the might of Rome for three years until, betrayed, they all perished: men, women, and children. The Jewish nation was destroyed and the Jews dispersed to the four corners of the earth.

As a land bridge between Africa and Asia and a port to the Mediterranean, Israel was a battleground for each. Babylonians, Assyrians, Romans, Greeks, Macedonians, Crusaders, Turks, British, a list as long as a river of blood.

Here is the Wadi 'Ara, a natural funnel through Israel. It has shaken beneath the tramping feet of a thousand invading armies. At the Wadi's end is Armageddon, where the last battle between good and evil will be fought.

In Israel the names on the land are as familiar as the names of our children. Who does not know of Ashkelon, of Samson and Delilah and Goliath and the Philistines?

Ruins left from Crusades and the Ottoman invasions linger on in the city of Jaffa, founded by the Phoenicians. It is the oldest port in the world.

And Roman ruins linger in Caesarea, for centuries the capital of tyranny.

There were benevolent tyrants, too, like Alexander the Great, for whom this stream is named. He was held in such esteem that as the Judaeo-Grecian cultures fused for years almost every male child was named Alexander.

Five thousand years of war have left little but desolation.

Broken walls . . . broken dreams of grandeur.

44

The captains and the kings depart.

A stone from the great Temple is all that is left.

Israel treats her past with reverence.

Her past is studied meticulously. Abda, a Nabataean City, was carved out of a mountainside for defense against men and protection against the blazing desert sun.

Hazor, a Canaanite city, was conquered by Joshua. It shows the scars of ancient battle, reaffirming the great accuracy of the Bible.

48

The dispersed Jews, destroyed as a nation, suffered unspeakable persecution in most of the world. They never stopped looking toward their ancient homeland with the prayer that ended, "Next year in Jerusalem."

After the Crusades, during the Ottoman era, a few pious ones managed to return to establish centers of religious study in Safed, Hebron, and Jerusalem.

About 1875, bloody anti-Jewish pogroms rocked Russia. A new kind of immigrant came to Palestine with the dream of reclaiming the country. This was the First Aliyah—the first immigration wave.

The "Land of Milk and Honey" had become a swamp.

The lush Judean hills of Biblical days had supported hundreds of thousands of people. Now the hills lay bleeding and fallow from neglect. Bony rocks of the ancient terracing poked through eroded, wasted earth.

The Jewish villages of the 1880s barely held their own. Jews knew little or nothing about farming and as little of fighting. There was an unjust Ottoman rule, and they were at the mercy of thieving bands of Bedouins.

52

As the massacre of Eastern European Jews heightened, the need for a Jewish homeland became increasingly obvious. Theodor Herzl's comet streaked over the sky with blinding light and speed. It was a mere ten years from the day he envisioned Zionism until he died of a heart attack from exhaustion at the age of forty-four.

In the first Zionist convention held in 1897 in Basle, Switzerland he wrote in his diary, "In Basle I established a Jewish State. If I were to say that aloud today, universal laughter would be the response. Maybe in five years, certainly in fifty, everybody will recognize it."

He is buried on Mount Herzl facing Jerusalem, the father of a country he never lived to see.

Other men slept facing Jerusalem who were not Zionists. The Baron
Rothschild, moved by the plight of his fellow Jews, poured tens of millions of
dollars into buying land and establishing villages.

In 1905 the Russian and Polish pogroms reached a new crescendo. The Second Aliyah came to Palestine filled with idealism. They moved into the swampland as quickly as it could be purchased.

Eucalyptus trees were imported from Australia to help drink up the malarial swamps.

56

The *kibbutz,* a voluntary communal farm, was the first positive answer to large-scale redemption and self-defense. Pioneers of the Second Aliyah waived material gain for a greater ideal, and after much trial and error, startling progress was made.

In World War I the Jews cast their lot with the British against the ruling Turks and suffered grievous persecution. Many were forced to flee but returned in the ranks of the victorious British Army.

The saga of the Aaronson family symbolized the era. They were a wealthy landowning family made up of poets, scientists, and dreamers, and served as agents for the British.

Sarah Aaronson was seized and held in her home in Zichron Yakov by the Turkish police.

She was strapped to her bed and tortured for information. She was lashed across the soles of her feet, and hot stones were placed under her armpits. She endured it for three days and three nights.

Nearly insane with pain she crawled to the bathroom, found a hidden pistol in the closet, placed the barrel in her mouth, and squeezed the trigger. Then she reeled into the tub . . . hung onto life for a few more tormented days . . . and died.

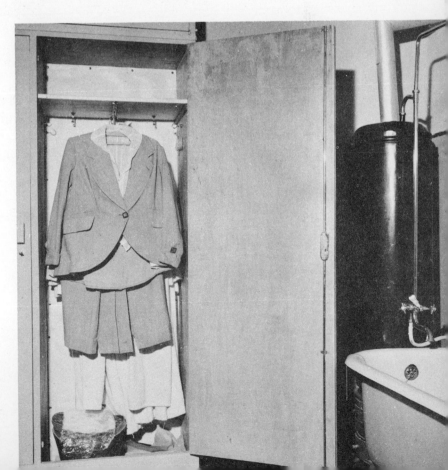

Ryfka Aaronson, sole survivor of the family and one of the last of Israel's landed gentry, preserves the role her family played in the history of her country.

At the end of World War I, Palestine became a British Mandate.

The Jews were given their "Magna Charta," the Balfour Declaration, a document favoring the establishment of a Jewish homeland in Palestine ratified by most of the civilized world.

Renewed anti-semitism in Eastern Europe triggered the Third Aliyah. The ensuing two decades saw enormous strides made.

Zionism had built a strong international machinery, and the Haganah, an army of self-defense, came into being.

61

Gigantic land deals were made. In one swoop the entire Jezreel Valley
was purchased.

The people of the Third Aliyah increased the rate of reclamation and redemption.

Forests were planted and roads were built . . .

. . . and railroads spanned the land.

64

Built on the ruins of tyrants, the *kibbutz* became a good way of life.

The *moshav* co-operative movement, which, unlike the *kibbutzim,* allowed private farms, also proved successful.

The new generation, which had been denied the right either to own or farm land in many of the countries of its dispersion, had to be rededicated to the soil after a two-thousand-year lapse.

68

A few decades ago most Jews did not know how to milk a cow.

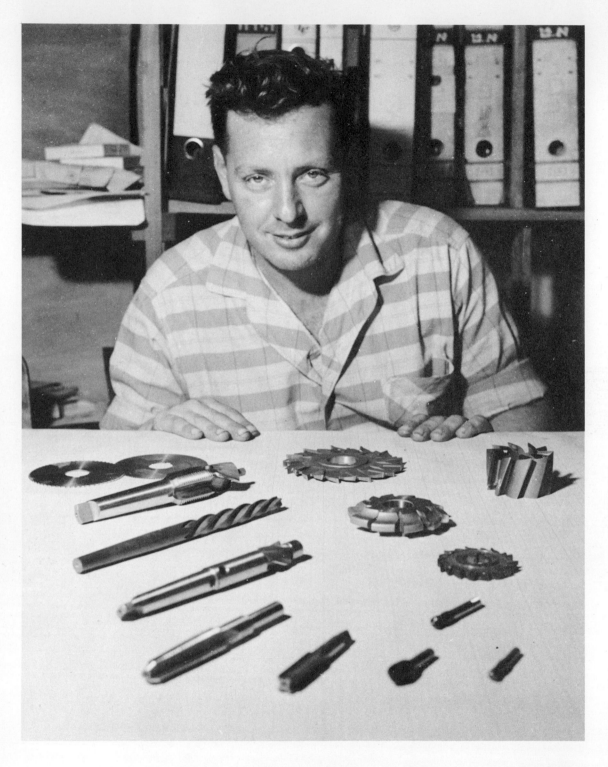

Many villages and *kibbutzim* took on light industry and found hundreds of new items to manufacture to augment their incomes.

Hebrew, the ancient language reserved for prayer, had an unprecedented revival. Never before had a "dead" tongue been brought back as a national spoken language. Today, it is taught in crash programs of the *ulpan* . . .

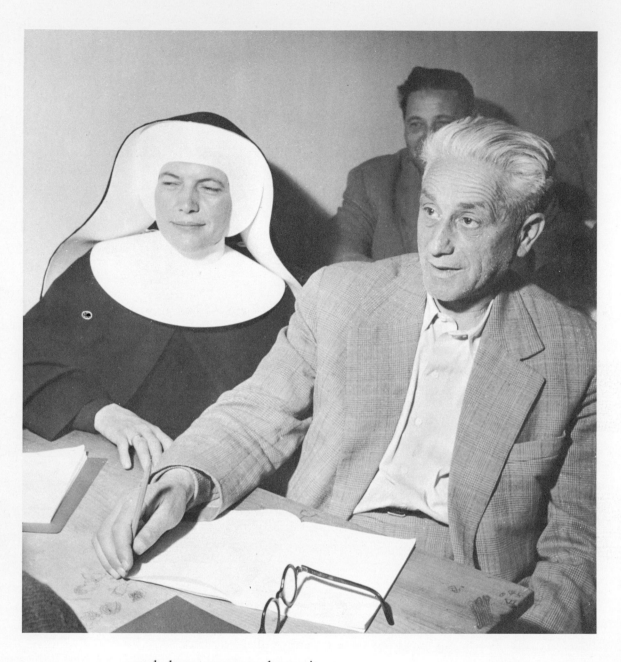

. . . and almost everyone learns it.

The Jews did not redeem Palestine without great cost in sacrifice and bloodshed.

Arab leaders, led by the Mufti of Jerusalem, constantly goaded the Arab community into riots and kept their people on the brink of hysteria.

The British, using Palestine as a political pawn, feared an Arab oil boycott and bowed to expediency. On occasion, they bowed to their conscience.

Turmoil, and a deepening morass of confusion, marked the twenties and burst into a full-blown pogrom in 1929.

The fever pitch was reached during the '30s as the German Aliyah began for those wise enough to flee Hitler.

The years 1936 through 1939 marked the Mufti-inspired Arab riots.

Now, tough and capable, the Jews still practiced patience through the Haganah, the army of self-defense, and the hope of ultimate justice at the conference tables.

In the Third Aliyah a new kind of Jew came into being—the fighter and the farmer. The native born were called *sabras,* after the fruit of the cactus which is tough and tender at the same time. To them fell the monumental task of leading the Jewish people to a status of dignity they had not known since the dispersion.

All Palestine became three armed camps. The British used a defense system similar to one used during the Crusades. Fifty Taggart forts spanned the tiny country.

And border blockhouses tried to stem Arab smuggling of arms and the crossing of terror bands.

As the Arab riots worsened, the Jews finally came out from hiding. The *kibbutz* of Hanita was built to block the path used by smuggler gangs from the Lebanon. The cream of Palestine's Jewish youth played "king on the hill" and defied the Arabs to throw them off. Many say that Israel was really born here whcrc the Jews held the high ground.

Not satisfied merely to hold a defensive position, the youngsters at Hanita dug roots and opened the door to "hill and terrace" farming.

Hanita became a base for the Night Raiders of the British Zionist officer, Orde Wingate. Quoting the Bible to his Jewish fighters, he led them on attacks of retribution against the Arabs. They struck with fury. The Arab rebellion collapsed.

During World War II the Jewish community went to war to a man and made a magnificent contribution to Allied victory.

The story of the Arab nations is sordid. From flirtation to overt declaration on behalf of the Nazis, they did next to nothing for Allied victory. Arab treachery reached a climax when the Mufti, instigator of most of Palestine's troubles, threw himself into Adolf Hitler's arms.

Despite the record, the British again bowed to Arab blackmail and blockaded the coast of Palestine against entry of the pathetic survivors of Hitler's policy of extermination.

The Haganah built for the inevitable showdown. The "battle of the conference tables" raged. In a less spectacular but important phase of the over-all battle, Illegal Immigration —Aliyah Bet—answered the British naval blockade.

It was however, the Jewish extremist underground, the Irgun Tsevai Leumi and the Stern Group, who dealt British and Arab devastating blows with their chilling war cry . . . "An eye for an eye!"

The Acre jail, toughest in the entire British penal system, was built in a Crusader fortress. It had walls ten feet thick.

Many of Palestine's Jews served time as "guests" of the British for their political, military, and underground activities. Their names were carved in defiance on the prison walls.

Some were acquainted with the death cells.

They said their last good-bys through a tiny barred window.

82

Dressed in the traditional scarlet hanging costume, they could hear the hangman prepare the gallows in the next room to assure a smooth execution.

The Jewish extremist underground planned their greatest action. It was dangerous, for Acre was an all-Arab city. They waited until it fell into a sizzling midday lethargy.

Some, dressed as Arabs and speaking Arabic, went into the mosque to "pray."

They slipped in and moved quickly and quietly to predetermined locations. One group strung out along the ancient sea wall.

Another group sat about on the ground in the khan, an old trading square...

. . . and along the waterfront . . .

. . . and on the ramparts.

As zero hour approached, they threaded their way in one direction.

They rushed the bathhouse and climbed to its roof. Here was the one blind spot on the prison. A charge of dynamite was attached to the wall and it blew! The British were caught napping. The raiders raced in and freed all the prisoners.

90

Many gave their lives in this venture, but it helped break the back of the Mandate. From the Acre raid, the British learned the extent of Jewish determination.

Less spectacular but equally effective, illegal immigration under the Haganah emptied Europe's refugee camps.

Then, the Haganah came from under wraps and harassed the British unmercifully.

No longer able to cope with the situation, the British left Palestine in humiliation. Like the other captains and kings they left little behind but bitter memories.

The question of the Palestine Mandate was thrown open to the United Nations. The bar of world justice judged that the Jewish people should be allowed to declare statehood in their ancient homeland. Once the decision was made, however, the Jews were abandoned. They had very little in the way of arms and faced the threat of extermination from seven Arab nations as well as the Arab community within Palestine.

In the face of this one of the most monumental events of our times took place.

On May 14, 1948, the Declaration of Independence for the State of Israel was proclaimed.

Within hours she was attacked by her Arab neighbors.

The War of Liberation which followed was unique. Infant Israel had to face her enemy on a thousand fronts. Each settlement was its own bastion, a potential Masada.

Each was ordered to hold . . . to hold without hope of arms or reinforcements . . . to hold while the army of Israel could grow . . . to hold against fantastic odds.

The saga of the settlements did justice to the great fighting tradition of the Biblical Hebrews.

Dagania, the first *kibbutz,* was a symbol to all of Israel. Unable to get either arms or reinforcements, empty trucks were run from Tiberias to Dagania to deceive the enemy. When attack was imminent they appealed to the high command for something to fight with. They were told, "Let the Syrians inside the *kibbutz*. When you see them on your land, you'll get so mad you'll get rid of them, somehow."

The Syrian attack penetrated into the *kibbutz* toward the inner defense around the children's houses. Livid with anger, a *kibbutznik* leaped atop the lead tank, opened the hatch, and threw in a Molotov cocktail. Galvanized into action, the farmers of Dagania attacked the enemy with rifles, pistols, knives, and pitchforks and threw him out.

95

Across the Sea of Galilee from Dagania, Ein Gev's geographical position gave Israel claim to the lake, and the holding of the *kibbutz* was vital.

At Ein Gev the land was farmed right up to the Syrian border. An enemy village hovered directly over them. The people of Ein Gev were subjected to a merciless artillery barrage, and they had nothing large enough to shoot back with.

Cut off by land, it received meager supplies at night by boat from Tiberias. The people moved underground and lived by day in their bunkers.

At night they came out and watered their fields.

The Syrians looked down their throats from the high ground. A half dozen attacks were beaten back. In the last one, the farmers of Ein Gev broke the Syrians with but eleven rounds of ammunition left.

Later, supplied and reinforced, they scaled the ancient Roman fort of Susita and in a surprise night attack threw their tormentors out. The battle of Ein Gev won the Sea of Galilee for Israel.

Ayelet Hashahar, another northern *kibbutz*, took a brutal pounding from Syrian guns but held its ground. A Syrian fighter plane was downed with a rifle shot. Every man in the *kibbutz* modestly takes credit for firing the shot.

Not all of the settlements held. Yad Mordechai sat on the Gaza Strip in the path of an Egyptian onslaught. It was isolated immediately.

Yad Mordechai withstood the siege for three months. Food was gone, water was gone, and the last round of ammunition had been fired. The Jews slipped out by night. The Egyptians entered and, after pillaging, burned every building to the ground. The Arabs soon learned that every Jewish village would have to be conquered at the cost of sustained, inch-by-inch fighting. They were able to take only a mere dozen.

Kibbutz Manara, in the Huleh Valley, was built on a mountaintop. It was isolated in a freezing winter under the siege of Iraqui irregulars, Lebanese, and Syrians.

Facing starvation, a desperate decision was made. One night the children were carried down the mountainside between enemy lines to the relative safety of the valley floor. The parents remained. Manara held.

Perhaps the most inspiring defense in the early days was Safed. Here the Jewish position was deemed impossible. Mount Canaan looks down on the Taggart fort and the citadel, which were both in Arab hands. As a base for Iraqui and Syrian irregulars, the town was loaded with heavily armed fighters. The Arab weapon superiority was a hundred to one. They outnumbered the Jews twenty-five to one. The Arabs held all the key positions. The Mufti announced his intention to make Safed his temporary capital on his "victorious return" to Palestine.

For centuries the Jews had looked upon Safed as a "capital in exile." It had been a center of religious study and filled with pious old Cabalists who were always the first victims of Arab riots.

Each house was an outpost. It was death to move in the streets. A narrow lane divided the Arab and Jewish sectors. The Jews dug in under siege conditions.

The gulf widened between the two quarters. Things were so bad on the Jewish side that the soldiers were fined for firing a bad round.

The Jews held on down to their last bag of flour. Letters with hand-made postage stamps, smuggled in and out during the night, were honored all over Israel.

108

Meivar, the Haganah commander, was born in Safed. "From childhood we cringed every time we heard the angry chanting start up in the Arab quarters. In 1929 and during the '36-'39 riots we hid in the old Turkish police fort. The Arab mobs went after the old Cabalists who couldn't fight back.

"This time we swore nothing was going to drive us out again. All during the siege no one thought of quitting. When things were darkest the Davidka —the Little David mortar—was sent to us, and a small reinforcement from the Palmach, the striking arm of the Haganah."

The Little David and the Palmach did the job. For several days the mortar blasted the Arab quarter with devastating effect. When the sky opened and it began to rain, the Jews spread the rumor that they had an atom bomb. The Arabs panicked. After a brief counter-offensive by the Palmach, Safed fell to the Jews.

The impossible had happened. After Safed, all the Arab strongholds in Galilee collapsed. One Israeli commander swears it was the most important victory of the war.

On other fronts Israel scored spectacular victories. Arab Jaffa and Jewish Tel Aviv squared off against each other. The Jewish line was held by Irgun Tsevai Leumi, the former underground extremist organization.

After a sharp and bitter encounter the defenses of Jaffa collapsed like a house of cards.

In Tiberias, the Haganah grabbed the Taggart fort and controlled most of the Sea of Galilee from the very beginning.

Haifa was one of the few places where the Jews held the high ground. Barrel bombs were rolled down the Carmel into the Arab quarters. Despite British help to the Arabs a catastrophic defeat loomed. The Haganah swept down the Carmel and took position after position. The Arab fate was sealed when a reinforcement convoy from the Lebanon was ambushed and chopped to pieces. The Jewish mayor of Haifa asked the Arabs to remain, but they were goaded by their leaders into flight.

Arab refugees from Haifa poured into Acre as the Haganah closed in from three sides. The city which had once stopped Napoleon's advance to India fell.

If the settlements were the backbone of Israel's defense, Jerusalem was the heart. Without Jerusalem there could really be no Israel.

A series of heights in the Judean hills held by Arab villages dominated a snaky road to Jerusalem called Bab el Wad. Convoys of homemade armored cars fought their way from Tel Aviv with supplies. Bab el Wad was littered with their wreckage of ambushes.

In the first offensive victory of the War of Liberation the Palmach threw the Arabs from one of the key heights, the Kastel.

But the road was plugged tight at a place called Latrun. The Jordanian Arab Legion mounted the walls of the Old City and poured withering gunfire into the Jewish sector.

The "no man's land" between Arab and Jewish Jerusalem was raked clean. Isolated Jewish Jerusalem was slowly being strangled.

Every street was a battlefield.

Kibbutz Ramat Rahel stood on the southern road to Bethlehem. Near the place where Rachel, the wife of Jacob, wept for the lost children of Israel, the Egyptians in order to enter Jerusalem from the south attacked. Ramat Rahel changed hands six times. The last victory belonged to the Army of Israel.

Then in anger and desperation wildcat Jewish attacks were launched from Mount Zion to try to force the Arab Legion from the Old City. They all failed.

One night a daring adventurer found an ancient Roman road through the *wadis* and Judean hills which bypassed the Arab stronghold of Latrun. Task forces from Tel Aviv and Jerusalem built a new road quickly and silently. It was called "the Burma Road."

At the instant the road builders from Tel Aviv and Jerusalem touched hands, Israel had won her war. The siege was lifted and Jerusalem was saved! The Army of Israel grew stronger and stronger and dealt the transgressors defeat after defeat.

Of all the epics, none is greater than the story of Negba. The Egyptian-held Taggart fort, Iraq Suweidan, was known as "the Monster on the Hill." It dominated key crossroads in the Negev Desert.

It was opposed by the *kibbutz* of Negba. From the rear of "the Monster on the Hill" the Egyptian guns rained a steady cannonade at point-blank range on the *kibbutz,* which had nothing large enough to return fire.

All that was left standing in Negba was the water tower . . .

and even that was useless.

Somehow Negba continued to hold for month after month. The Egyptian assault came led by seven tanks. The Jews had but thirteen rounds of anti-tank ammunition. That was all they needed. The Egyptians never reached the front gate.

One day the Army of Israel threw the enemy from "the Monster on the Hill." In the ensuing action nearby a young Egyptian captain named Gamal Abdul Nasser learned the might of Israel—but not well enough.

The spirit of Negba and of Negbas all over Israel was too much for the Arabs. They were driven beyond the borders of Israel forever.

At Tel Hai is a national shrine: the graves of the first guardsmen who defended Jewish villages at the turn of the century.

The Lion of Tel Hai looks down upon the fulfillment of a prophecy.

128

Book Two

Israel is a sound of laughter! In Purim week it finds its greatest expression. This time of gaiety commemorates the ancient Queen Esther who saved her people from an early-day Hitler, the Amalekite Haman.

The spectators at the big parade are as interesting as the parade.

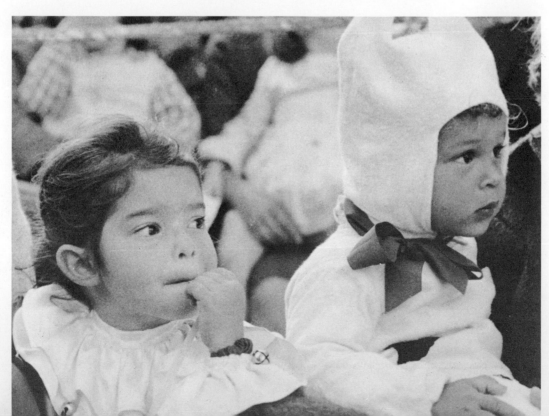

Santa Claus?

It takes a stern but kindly
cop to hold back the crowds.

132

The people of Israel are aware that Stewart Granger is faster than the fastest gun alive.

Only a Greek photographer would spot the one child in Greek costume among the hundred thousand plus spectators.

It was a fine parade.

Israel in her three great cities, each unique unto itself.
Fifty years ago a sand dune stood on the edge of Jaffa.
Today . . .

Tel Aviv.

The architecture is striking.

At the Habima, the National Theater, you can see *Death of a Salesman*
in Hebrew and translations of Shaw and Shakespeare or maybe the premiere
of one of Israel's several new and vital playwrights.

The home of the Israel Philharmonic Orchestra, led in its debut perform-
ance by the late Arturo Toscanini.

Histadrut, the labor organization indispensable in the building of Israel, has its headquarters housed in Tel Aviv's largest building.

I liked Tel Aviv best because I am a big city boy, but who can deny the breathtaking beauty of Haifa? The most wonderful tribute I know is that it is called "Little San Francisco." Harissiadis favored Haifa—it reminded him of Athens.

The unique oil refinery, once a scene of riots and terrorism, is the first in a chain of heavy industrial plants that follow the arc of the bay from Haifa to Acre.

The new Jerusalem is hewn from that odd pink "Jerusalem" stone blasted from the Judean hills. Ilan Hartuv, the third man on our team, is a Jerusalemite. He is a complete chauvinist about his city.

It is filled with striking modern structures like the Convention Hall which has lured international conclaves.

Moish Pearlman is the "Grover Whalen" of Israel.

Jerusalem is the heart of Judaism. Here the Jewish tragedy is recorded. At Yad Vashem on Mount Herzl the murder of six million Jews by the Nazis is documented. In these files are catalogued the epitome of man's inhumanity to man.

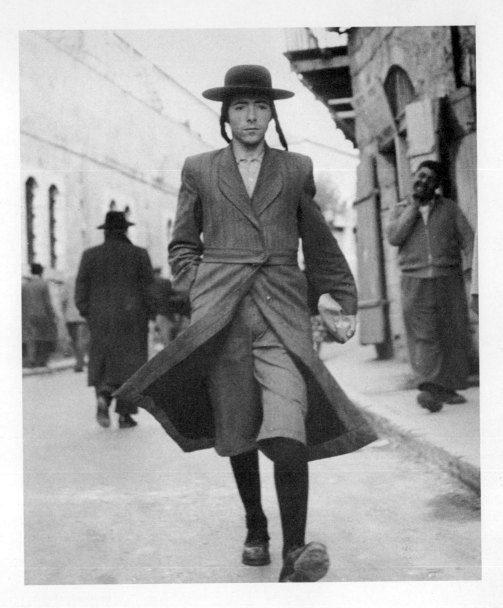

In Jerusalem there are sects of pious fanatics who live in the past.

Some do not even recognize the existence of the State of Israel, or much else for that matter. They are treated with an inexhaustible patience.

Their lives center around study
of the Torah and prayer.

148

These sects were born out of anguish as the result of massacres during the Middle Ages. They found hope through frenzied prayer.

Strangers are treated with suspicion.

They live with a strict adherence to the letter of the Torah . . . the shaved
heads of the married women . . . the ritual bath . . . the minute interpretations
of the "*law*."

150

"Does the book not say that King David will return to earth as the Messiah and reclaim Israel? What utter nonsense have these new people brought with them?"

The things which endear Jerusalem to most of mankind are timeless: the Mount of Olives, Gethsemane, the Dome of the Rock, the Wailing Wall, the Valley of Kidron ... Zion.

The Sanhedrin tombs: the graves of men who constituted one of the world's first democratic courts.

154

On Mount Zion is the site of the Last Supper and of Mary's dormition.
And the tomb of King David. Jerusalem is *still* the City Of David.

Jerusalem gives a feeling of sadness. It is most intense at the break
of dawn when the voice of the muezzin drifts over the ethereal stillness from
the Old City, calling the Moslems to prayer . . .

for Jerusalem is divided in half at the Mandelbaum Gate.

Traffic is light on this street. A few pilgrims at Christmas and Easter . . .
United Nations personnel who stop here to change their license plates from
Jordanian to Israeli . . . sometimes in Mandelbaum Square families separated
by the war a decade ago are allowed to meet for a few moments and weep in
each other's arms.

A Canadian and New Zealander in the Mixed Armistice Commission said,
"The tension has eased. Incidents are becoming rare."
Nevertheless . . .

Israel's frontier
is at the end of a street.

As the cry of the muezzin ends the silence of night, Jew and Arab long for that day when Jerusalem will again be one. Until then, the United Nations looks down from a place known since Biblical days as "the Hill of Evil Council," where Judas sold out Christ for forty pieces of silver.

160

Israel is her Bedouins. No people hold greater mystery and fascination than those who wander the desert. They seem still plagued by an ancient curse of Abraham who cast Hagar and Ishmael to the cruel mercy of the wasted expanses.

All life is an eternal and almost fruitless search for water.

They have little save the rags on their backs.

The life of privation is indelibly etched on their faces.

Not even the amulet to ward off the "evil eye" helps much.

163

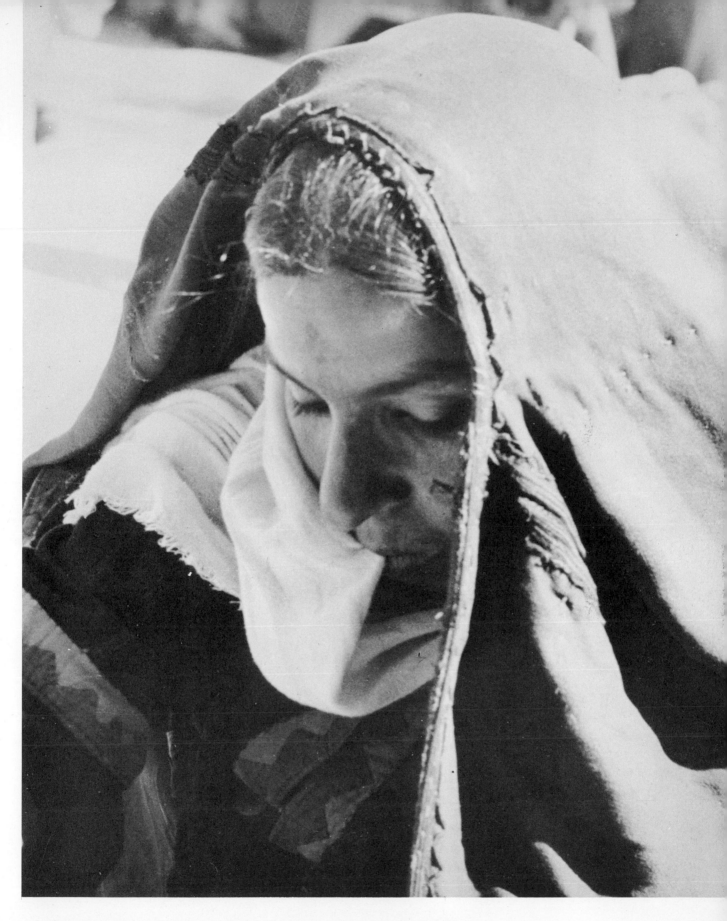

Yet, through it all, they maintain a strange and wonderful dignity
and a belief in their freedom.

A traveler is never turned away . . .

and they are the most magnificent
of hosts.

Sheik Aude Abou Amar has a crafty mind as keen as the blade of his dagger. Israel, somehow, has made him different from other sheiks. He wants water for his people and he dreams of that day they will have homes of stone and cease their aimless wandering.

He has made the first of many long and difficult steps that someday will bring his people into a modern world.

Beersheba—the Seven Wells, the City of Abraham. Each Thursday since time immemorial, thousands of Bedouins appear from nowhere for the day of barter.

Bargains are thoroughly discussed.
With concentration and shrewdness one sizes up the merchandise.

170

Decisions are a family affair.

All transactions are weighed carefully.

One must not show anxiety, for barter requires great patience and skill . . .

. . . and no one is in a hurry.

Suddenly the evening falls . . .

. . . and they vanish into the desert.

In America, Druse Kammel Mansour was decked out in full tribal regalia and in the "isolation booth" of the "$64,000 Question." An official in Minority Affairs, this is his normal "costume."

Israel is a land of crooked alleys . . .

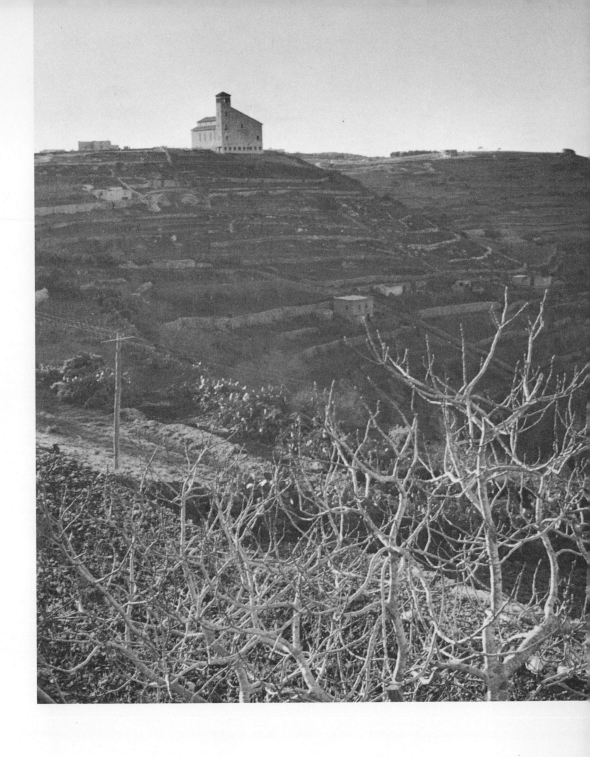

. . . and picturesque places . . .

. . . and picturesque people . . . big . . .

. . . and little . . .

... and many kinds of people ...

in many kinds of places.

Israel can be a photographer's nightmare for there are those who believe
a camera is an "evil eye." . . .

...or a "graven image."

Israel has kept faith with that Jewish tradition which has always paid the greatest homage to its learned.

It is fitting that Israel's first president was a scientist.

Chaim Weizmann's monument, the Weizmann Institute, is a city of research. There is nothing else like it in the Middle East.

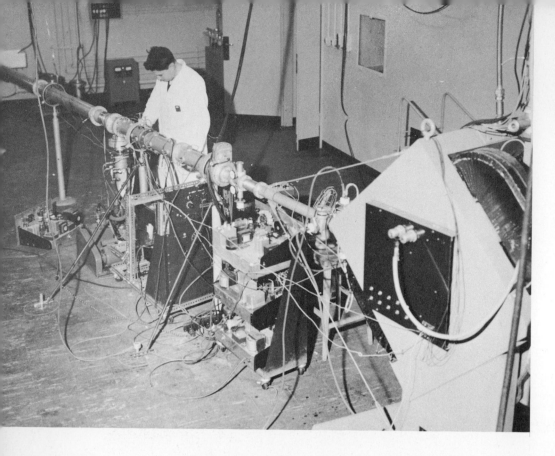

Here is Israel's first nuclear reactor. In this city of research they seek the cause of cancer, they learn how to use solar energy, they are far advanced in methods of converting sea water to fresh water. A hundred diversified programs are carried on.

Swiss-born Dr. Mathilda Krim is a co-discoverer of the method to determine sex of embryo.

Institute Head Meyer Weisgal stands before a map of planned expansion, Yad Chaim Weizmann—the monument to Chaim Weizmann. It will solidify the Institute's position among the foremost centers of science in the world.

On Mount Carmel in Haifa another center of science is being built—a city of engineers.

The Churchill Auditorium is in the center of Technion City. From here
will come Israel's future mechanical, civil, and electrical engineers.

The central link in Israel's chain of knowledge is Hebrew University. Denied the use of their campus on Mount Scopus, men of vision would not be deterred.

This is the new Hebrew University, crowning symbol of Jerusalem!

Here the challenge of statehood is answered in medicine, law, the humanities, social sciences, economics, agriculture and research.

The varied curriculum has lured students of all kinds from all parts of the world.

Love of knowledge is not the exclusive property of the great institutions.

The walls of the most humble homes are lined with books. A *kibbutz* with a few hundred members will probably have a library of several thousand volumes in a half dozen languages.

At Ein Gev, night concerts are given on the Sea of Galilee to augment the *kibbutz* income. Every major artist coming to Israel plays an engagement in this huge auditorium.

A museum, a research lab, an agricultural experimentation station, a center of science or art like the A. D. Gordon House in Dagania *kibbutz* are commonplace everywhere.

194

Israel is a symphony of progress keynoted by the Nesher cement factory which closes only twenty-four hours a year, on Yom Kippur, the Day Of Atonement.

Since the Israelis were shut out of their hospital on Mount Scopus, a new medical center races toward completion. The Hadassah Medical Center in Ein Karem, birthplace of John the Baptist, will be the largest building in the Middle East and take its place as a city of medicine alongside the cities of engineers and research scientists.

The sound of building never stops. There must be homes for a population which has tripled in a decade. Gone are the tent cities. Vanishing are the ugly tin shacks of temporary housing for new immigrants.

196

Constant experimentation has made Israel nearly self-sufficient in food. The search for new products never ends. This is a field of sisal hemp from Mexico planned for a future industry for the manufacture and export of rope.

Israel is her people, who have come from eighty different countries.

Many of the new pioneers are businessmen.

Others have memories imprinted on their minds . . . and tattooed on their arms.

For the descendants of the survivors of Hitler, all of Europe had become a coffin.

At the end of World War II they beat their way to Palestine in leaky tugboats and beached themselves on her shores in defiance of the British naval blockade . . .

And they braved new concentration camps, British style . . .

And carved for themselves a life of dignity away from the shadow of oppression . . .

. . . a life without barbed wire where the word, "Jew," does not have an ugly meaning . . .

203

. . . a life without second-class citizenship, slander, bigotry, and Nazi barbarism . . .

204

. . . a life without fear and without hunger.

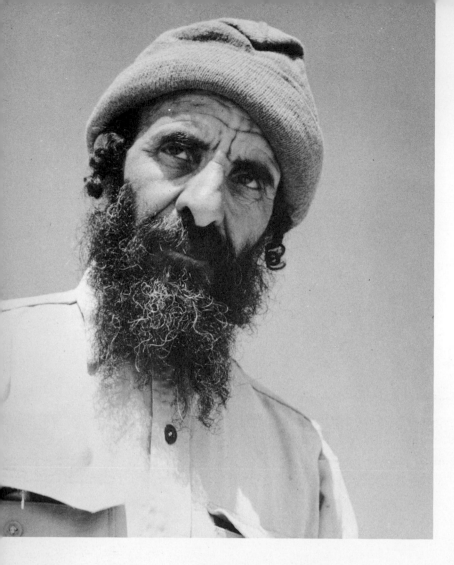

Nearly every immigrant has a strange and awesome story. None is more strange or more awesome than that of the Yemenites. Two thousand years ago they left Israel to establish a trading colony in the Land of Sheba.

They lived in isolation from civilization. Through a long and tortured history of persecution they never lost their identity as Jews on pain of death.

When they learned that "David had returned to Jerusalem" they marched through hundreds of miles of wild country and burning sand at the mercy of cutthroat marauders. They marched with nothing more than the shirts on their backs and their Holy Torah Scrolls in their arms. They arrived at the Crown Colony of Aden looking like characters from the Old Testament.

When they saw their first airplane, they merely shrugged and pointed to that place in the Bible which told them they would mount up on wings as eagles and return to the Promised Land.

206

Israel is her children. All children have something in common.
Jewish children . . .

. . . and Arab children.

The children of Israel are intelligent . . .

. . . alert . . .

. . . and inquisitive.

210

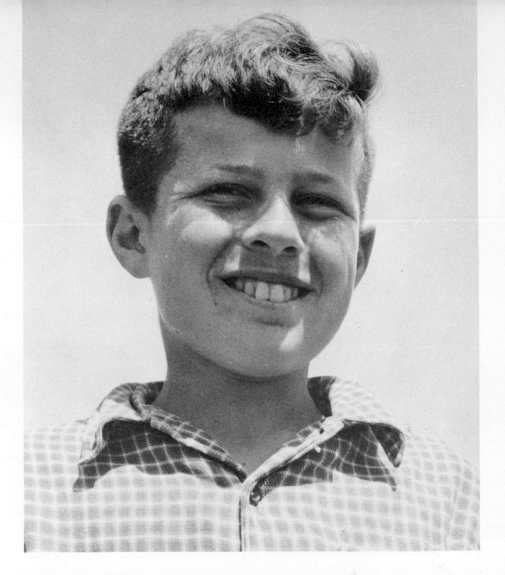

They come in singles . . .

and in pairs . . .

. . . and a variety of shades that have made Israel a showcase of democracy.

They march the length and the breadth of their land singing...from
Mount Zion...

. . . to the Galilee and up Tabor, where Deborah, the first Joan of Arc, swept down on the Canaanite host.

Children like these were once in German extermination camps.

After centuries of darkness, the Arab children begin to ask the questions that free men want answered.

A Bedouin boy was found dying in an alley in Beersheba by the foreman of the Abda excavation and nursed back to health. He proudly refused our offer of compensation for guiding us through the ruins. Israel has given him dignity, too.

A very few Jews cling to the ways of the ghetto.

But Israel pins her hopes on her tough and wonderful *sabras*.

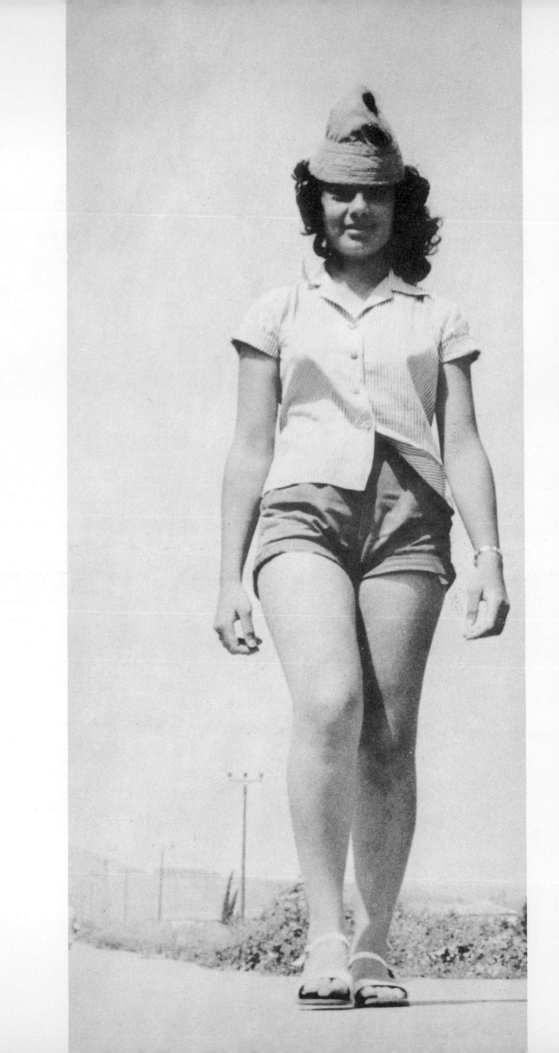

Israel is the strange and complex Arab. Is there an Arab problem in Israel? Of course there is. The Arabs are torn by the plight of loved ones who once fled beyond the borders. Despite equality under law they are not given to feel the complete sense of belonging to Israel. Only a peace treaty can solve that.

Betrayed by their leaders, they stampeded beyond the border. Their villages have decayed from neglect. Other refugees, Jewish refugees of Arab persecution, have taken their place.

Many of the old generation are unable to adapt to a modern society...

...and the world passes them by.

And many are trapped in a maze of superstition as ancient as this olive grove planted by the Romans.

Those who remained in Israel have a prosperity they have never known before.

They see tap water and electricity in their villages. In all of the Arab world they are the only ones who enjoy this degree of compulsory education, woman suffrage, health facilities, economic betterment.

They are being represented by progressive leaders such as Farras Hamdan, formerly a member of the Israel Parliament.

225

In the village of Baqa, where he is mayor, the new hospital sees to it that no more Arab women need die in childbirth. Tuberculosis, once a scourge, is all but vanished.

A joint Arab-Jewish business venture has eliminated unemployment in Baqa with a citrus canning factory.

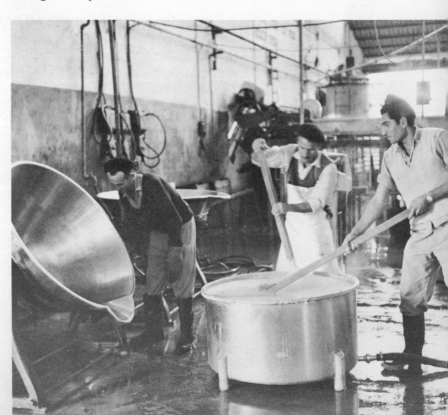

As Hamdan speaks to his Jewish foreman on expansion plans . . .

. . . the Arabs of Israel begin to find their way into the twentieth century.

Sabra means native born. Not all the *sabras* in Israel are Jewish. These *sabras* will demand a better way of life and complete participation in the life of their country, and Israel will give it to them.

Someday peace will bring a better life to all the Arabs of the Middle East.

Yosef Zeinabi on the right is a member of the only Jewish family which has farmed the land consecutively since the fall of the Temples. To withstand the massacres through the ages, the Zeinabi family has been protected by their Moslem, Christian, and Druse neighbors.

Here, Christian, Druse, and Jew sit together on the town council of Peki'in and plan for a better future together.

Israel is the challenge of the desert. Scorched . . .

. . . brooding . . .

. . . vast.

In the greatest of all paradoxes, Israel looks back to the Wilderness of
Zin for her future.

Somewhere there are minerals . . .

Somewhere there is oil.

Something new has been added to ancient Beersheba...

234

... a base camp for scientists and engineers .

and an occasional itinerant writer.

In the dynamic rebirth of Israel the use of applied science has lured the greats and not so greats from all over the world. At the Hias House you are apt to run into a variety of people from Edward G. Robinson to some obscure oil wildcatter.

Here is one of the greats.

Dr. Ernst Chain won a Nobel Prize for the co-discovery of penicillin. He was denied knighthood, which Fleming received, because he is a Jew.

Another base at the head of the desert is the Dagon Hotel in Ashkelon—former stamping ground of Samson and Delilah.

Water is the key to life in the desert. To divert the northern rivers in gigantic water schemes, the largest pipe factory of its kind in the world was constructed at the head of the desert . . .

. . . by machines . . .

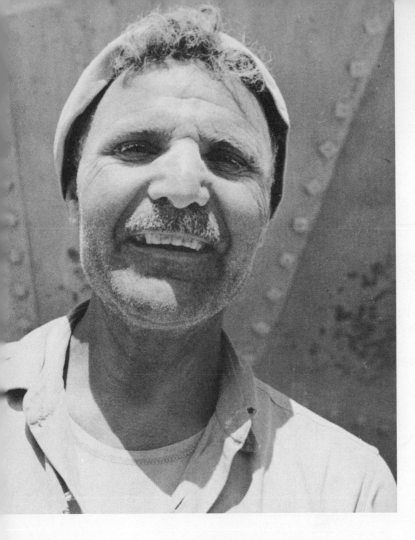

. . . and men.

As the rivers will be moved south . . .

. . . highways are carved through the wilderness.

It takes a hardy breed of desert rats to conquer land which has never given life to so much as a blade of grass.

Pioneers build villages on the brink of hell . . .

and there is a harvest in the desert.

Teams of archaeologists join the geologists in scouring the desert for hidden treasure. Using clues in the Bible, they have tracked down mineral deposits known to ancient kings. At Timna, the smelting pits of King Solomon's copper mines were found . . .

244

. . . and after a lapse of two thousand years the mines were reopened.

Phosphate is mined in the Ramon Crater, and potash is being taken from the Dead Sea, where it has been stored untouched for millenniums. To move this to the world markets, Israel needed a southern port. Ten years ago all that stood here was this mud hut.

This is the "wild south." The pioneer town of Elath at the junction of Egypt, Israel, Jordan, and Saudi-Arabia is the world's newest port city in a country that has the world's oldest. Once the Red Sea opened for the wandering tribes of Israel. It is open again as potash pours out to revitalize the lands of potash-starved Asia.

Israel, with unshakable faith in the Bible, has translated the wisdoms of her prophets into this dynamic nation. Israel will conquer the desert as she has conquered the swamps and the erosion.

Israel is the Lions of Judah, reborn, the new Samsons and Joshuas and Davids.

Yigal Allon was born and raised as a farmer. The price of survival made him a soldier from boyhood. Before the age of thirty he commanded the Palmach, the striking arm of the Haganah.

At the age of thirty-one he was a general in the Army of Israel in command of the Southern Front, which swept the Negev in the War of Liberation.

Today he serves Israel as a Member of Parliament. He lives in Genossar, a fishing *kibbutz* on the Sea of Galilee.

Behind him is framed the Arbel, a fortress of the Maccabees, heroes of another age.

His daughter ran to him and cried, "Abba! Abba! The fishing boats are coming in!"

They walked off toward the jetty.

"I had to take a world trip recently and I'm away in Jerusalem most of the week. I don't see enough of the children."

He hopes for that day when the burdens of office will ease and he can resume his life as a fisherman.

Aaron Remez, former Member of Parliament, was the first commander of Israel's Air Force at the age of thirty. "In the beginning we had a striking power of three Piper Cubs. Our first bombardier was a girl who threw homemade hand grenades out of the window."

Yigael Yadin is a Jerusalemite. He is translator of the Dead Sea Scrolls discovered by his father, the late E. L. Sukenik. Like all Jerusalemites, Yadin carries an inseparable love for his city. As a young man he became a leader in the Haganah. With the declaration of statehood he became Chief of Operations of Israel's Army and later Chief of Staff in his early thirties.

Yadin has another love . . . archaeology. At the Hebrew University he explains the finds of the excavations of Hazor, the Canaanite city conquered by Joshua. "When the city was razed we found that the fire lines on the stones were accurately described in the chapters of Joshua."

252

Dan Ram was a hero of Hanita, the *kibbutz* built on the Lebanese border to halt the Arab uprising of 1936–1939. Ram later fought in the British Army in the invasion of Syria, and during Israel's War of Liberation was on the central intelligence staff. He still lives at Hanita and recalls the days when it was a base for the legendary Night Raiders of Orde Wingate and he crossed into the Lebanon in the first offensive actions the Jews took against their enemies.

254

This man is a living legend. He is Itzak Zuckerman, known as Antek. A Commander in the Warsaw ghetto uprising, he and his comrades staged the first rebellion against the Nazis and sounded the great trumpet that signaled the return of the Jewish people to their Biblical tradition as great fighters.

255

We were fortunate that Ilan Hartuv could join our team. He wore many hats from translator to travel agent to red-tape cutter. We could not have made the journey without him. His concentration was absolute as he translated Antek's story without missing a word.

We only had three hundred fighters armed with a few dozen rifles and pistols. Mostly homemade grenades, fire bombs, and knives. The Germans marched into the ghetto singing. They came to a halt at Zamenhoff and Mila streets. It was the way we figured . . . right into our trap. They sat about while their officers discussed their first moves. Our man who was to give the "open fire" signal was on a rooftop overlooking them. His hand was shaking with fright so badly he couldn't light his bottle bomb . . . and to make it worse, the wind blew out his matches. He finally lit the wick and hurled the bottle. It hit a German on the helmet and turned him into a torch. We opened a cross fire. They fled from the ghetto in terror, leaving their dead and wounded littered on the streets. That was the first day. For the next week we trapped them again and again and even stopped their tanks. Then it became hell. They lay back and bombarded us around the clock and knocked the ghetto down, brick by brick. Then they set it afire and used poison gas. They tortured children before the eyes of their mothers to get information on our bunker locations. They hounded us down with dogs, then filled the bunkers with poison gas. We hung on for forty-two days and forty-two nights. Not bad when you consider that the entire country of Poland held for only twenty-six.

Our week of interviews at the Fighters of the Ghetto *kibbutz* came at the end of four thousand kilometers of hard travel. I was transfixed as Ilan translated the story of Ziviah Lubetkin.

Ziviah is a heroine of the Warsaw uprising. She was not smiling when she told me her story.

When I reached the command bunker it was destroyed. Everyone had been killed by poison gas. The Germans had the ghetto in flames. There were fifty of us left in the Franceskanska Bunker. We had no food or water . . . ammo was about gone. We decided to take to the sewers.

258

In some places the water was near boiling from the heat of the fire above. For twelve hours we moved inch by inch in the kannals in pitch blackness holding hands in a chain ... no one spoke. At times the pipe grew small and we had to crouch for several hundred yards ... other times we moved on hands and knees. Sometimes the pipe got huge and we had to walk on tiptoes in neck-high sewage.

We got to the designated manhole and waited for help. We waited ... and waited ... and waited ... thirty-six hours passed. We could hear children playing on the street above. One man went insane from thirst and drank the sewer water. He was dead in minutes.

I kept telling myself ... "I'm going to survive ... I'm going to survive ... I'm going to live and see Israel."

Antek and Ziviah were married during the early days of the war in Poland. Today they live on the Fighters of the Ghetto *kibbutz* with their two strong and handsome *sabra* children.

259

Not all of Israel's heroes carried guns. For decades the brilliant Chaim Weizmann fought the battle of the conference tables with breath-taking skill. Vera Weizmann, Israel's First Lady, stands before the portrait of her late husband.

From his desk came the wisdom and statesmanship vital in winning Israel. It is said that Weizmann could argue a leopard out of his spots.

Weary but victorious, Chaim Weizmann died. The clock is stopped at the moment of his death. The Bible remains opened to that verse he was reading prophesying the coming of Israel.

For eight years after the War of Liberation, the Arab neighbors licked their wounds and swore vengeance. Israel was not allowed a moment of peace. The enemy lurked on every side.

Another generation had to be asked to live on the borders and stop the Arab fedayeen murder bands . . .

And another generation is forced to live with a gun pointed at its head.

Houses facing the enemy are surrounded by concrete walls. As in ancient days they worked their fields with one hand on the plowshare while the other held a spear.

Murder by trained bands, the repeated boast of extermination, and watching Arab armed might grow until the peril was imminent. Israel struck first. With the wrath of God in her soul, Israel crossed into the Sinai and obliterated the Egyptian Army.

A watchful waiting has developed. Hartuv looks down on Kiryat Shemona, a town where he once served as mayor. Since Sinai it has grown steadily.

The Notre Dame School looks down into the Old City of Jerusalem.
Once the scene of a raging battle . . . it is still the site of . . . watchful waiting.

Those on the border breathe a little easier. A few years ago I attended the funeral of a boy murdered here in Nahal Oz by fedayeen sent from Gaza on the horizon.

"Since Sinai" the Arab neighbors in more sober moments know that Israel is here to stay. Enlightened Arabs know that peace with Israel is the key to the alleviation of the suffering of their own people.

On the Gaza Strip, a United Nations check post watches patiently for that moment the Arab leaders will purge their hearts of blind hatred.

Arab women scratch a pathetic existence from the earth which could be made lush and green . . . as it has been made green on the other side of the border.

Someone else watches. The tough little Army of Israel watches. They will again turn Arab aggression into Arab disaster.

The *sabras* who have known little but bloodshed and sacrifice sometimes get restless and feel confined and need to go away from Israel for a time.

"Do you know what it is like to wake up in the morning in a place where the border is not in danger? Where you can listen to the news without hearing a threat to destroy you? Do you know what it's like? I guess you don't."

But the *sabras* all seem to return. They seem predestined by a greater power to the saving of their fellow Jews.

271

And each day a new young Lion of Judah takes his place in the ranks.

We . . .

274

. . . shall . . .

. . . not . . .

. . . perish!

No leader of our times, with the possible exception of Gandhi, has lived closer to his people than the twentieth-century prophet, David Ben Gurion.

In a tent of the paratroops in the Negev Desert, David Ben Gurion conducts the Passover Seder.

The youngest soldier present, reading from the ancient Haggadah, asks the question, "Why is this night different from all other nights of the year?"

Ben Gurion, father of the new House of David, answers, "This night is different because we celebrate the most important moment in the history of our people. On this night we celebrate the going forth in triumph from slavery to freedom."

Israel is the light of a new dawn.

As in ancient days, she is again a bridge from the world of darkness to the world of light.

DIMITRIOS HARISSIADIS

Born in Kavala, Greece, in 1911, Dimi was a chemist by training. He was always enchanted by photography and showed such proficiency as an amateur that between 1933 and 1940 dozens of his pictures ended up in international exhibitions.

He started his professional career as a roving free lancer and later became a portrait photographer. This was an era of mediocrity.

In World War II, Dimi served as a private in the Greek Army on the Albanian front and was made corps photographer by virtue of the fact that he was the only soldier to disobey regulations by putting a camera in his knapsack.

During the German Occupation he undertook the hazardous job of recording the destitution and starvation for the International Red Cross. His photos had to be smuggled from the country.

Since the war his assignments have included work for the United States Information Service, Associated Press, CARE, the United Nations, the Queen's Fund, and the ECA. He organized the photographic section of the Anglo-Greek Information Service and has served as staff newsreelman for CBS in Greece. In the latter field, he has shot several documentary films, including work for the Greek Tourist Bureau.

Recently, in the Art Institute of Chicago exhibition of the best of Greek photography, thirteen out of forty-two photographs were his.

His hobby is his work and the collection of folk music.

The acknowledged master in Greece, Dimi's pictures have appeared in most American magazines at one time or another and he is the only Greek photographer represented in the great *Family of Man*.

Leon Uris

PHOTOGRAPHING ISRAEL
by Dimitrios Harissiadis

The biggest problem in photographing Israel was Leon Uris. Don't travel with well-known authors. We planned our days with the best of intentions to start at, say, 0800, but Uris was always hung up on the phone and had to push through so many autograph hunters, amateur literary critics, newspapermen, and what not it was sometimes 1100 before we reached our car and then had to race for a luncheon appointment.

Uris expected me to take photographs; set exposures, focus, and shoot in about the same time it takes Gregory Peck to draw on a cattle rustler. He also expects you to take your shots from inside a fast-moving car moving over a bumpy road.

But Uris had his compensations. Occasionally he volunteered to carry a gadget bag or hold the flash.

In Israel one can photograph anywhere almost without restriction, even on the uneasy borders. The approaching border guard would always suggest better ways and means for you to do the job with the greatest safety.

Most people have no objection to being photographed and in fact ask to have their pictures taken. However, this is counter-balanced by those who do object to being photographed; such as certain Orthodox Jewish sects and the Moslem, Druse, and Bedouin women. I had to use every trick I knew to get their pictures. I shot over my head and backwards, sideways, stationed myself in a hidden place, used telephoto and even had Uris act as decoy. The Jewish Mea Shearim section of Jerusalem was particularly difficult as the inhabitants were wise to the ways of photographers. Here, the Rolleiflex proved invaluable. I was able to cradle it in my hand and let my arm hang naturally and press the shutter with my right thumb. Of course my position had to be fixed with the exposure and distance set in advance. Safest speed for this kind of work is 1/250.

Light in Israel is excellent. Sun is plentiful. However, for landscapes and clarity of atmosphere in long-distance work I would not recommend spring-time. We ran into a distressing amount of haze and moisture, especially in the Galilee. Autumn, with its cool air and grounded moisture would be far better.

There are no special problems for exposure evaluation if you have a good meter and some experience in its use. Many amateurs believe that meters behave differently in different countries. Visitors to Greece often ask if they should correct their meter readings because of the extreme intensity of the light. I assure them, and you, the meter isn't being fooled. However, the best and most accurate instrument should not be followed blindly. Readings should be interpreted according to existing conditions. Beersheba and the desert, for example, are bathed in flat, white, shadowless light. I underexposed the reading and overdeveloped slightly in order to increase contrast and gradation of negative. The reverse should be done on contrast subjects such as a narrow village street with patches of strong light and deep shadows. But this is not peculiar to Israel. The same would hold true in the whitewashed villages of Greek Islands as well as the dark forests of Switzerland.

Equipment and material are a personal matter. I almost hesitate to list mine, as one man's meat can be another man's poison.

Most of the shots were taken with a Rolleiflex f:3.5 Planar on Kodak Tri-X film. I used this fast film in anticipation of working under fast and variable conditions. Generally I prefer a slower film as Verichrome-Pan. The two extra stops of the Tri-X allowed me fast shutter speeds and small apertures for mobility and good depth of focus. Moreover, I confess I am not a fine-grain maniac. I've blown up these Israel pictures for exhibition and there is some grain in the 50 by 60cm sizes, but the lively subject matter amply justifies it to reasonable people.

In the matter of filters I used orange and medium yellow for long- and medium-range work but no filters in the close shots of people.

About 30 per cent of the pictures were taken with a Hasselblad which I switched to when I wanted a lens of focal length different from the 75mm Planar or the Rollei. This is a slower camera to set than the Rollei, but the advantages of wide-angle and telephoto lenses are obvious. I have equipped my Hasselblad with four lenses: a wide-angle 60mm, f:5.6 Distagon; a normal 80mm f:2.8 Tessar; a medium telephoto of 135mm f:3.5 Sonnar and a telephoto 250 mm f:4 Sonnar. Apart from the telephoto and wide-angle advantages, the Tessar lens came in handy for normal shooting when my Rollei shutter broke down in the Negev Desert. The breakdown was due to sand filtration because I carried the camera without its leather case for the sake of quick film changes. After this experience I don't recommend this procedure for dusty trips.

The film used in the Hasselblad was also Tri-X.

For color work I used a Retina IIc with a 50mm f:2.8 Retina-Xenon lens whose front element can be interchanged with the front element of a 35mm f:5.6 wide-angle Retina-Curtar-Xenon. The film used was Kodachrome Daylight.

Two Weston Master III exposure meters and a light Babyblitz-B electronic flash unit completed my equipment.

I took no tripod, guessing there would be no time to use it. I guessed right.

We traveled some 4000 kilometers in five weeks and I shot about 1200 negatives, of which 826 are now in my files. Such massive production invariably results in careless shooting, but the gods were good to me.

The co-ordination of Ilan Hartuv, his guidance and companionship made the trip a success as well as a pleasure. His knowledge of Israel is vast and absolute.

I must even reluctantly thank Uris, despite those wasted mornings when the sun was low and the shadows long and photogenic. He was a wonderful companion and astute observer who knew what he wanted.

Israel? My impressions could fill a dozen volumes. My greatest thrill was that moment Ben Gurion took me by the hand and led me behind his desk and asked me to translate from the original Greek the lines of Aeschylus on the principles of victory.

As I photographed the Mediterranean I realized that these very same waters had been breaking on the shores of my own beloved Greece and how the past history of the Greek and Jewish people, their disasters and glories, their gifts to mankind, are so similar.

Shalom. What a wonderful word for a greeting. To all the wonderful friends I made in Israel I hope this wayward Greek photographer has done justice to your warm, hospitable people and your magnificent country.

Shalom, Le'hitraot.